WONDER WALK

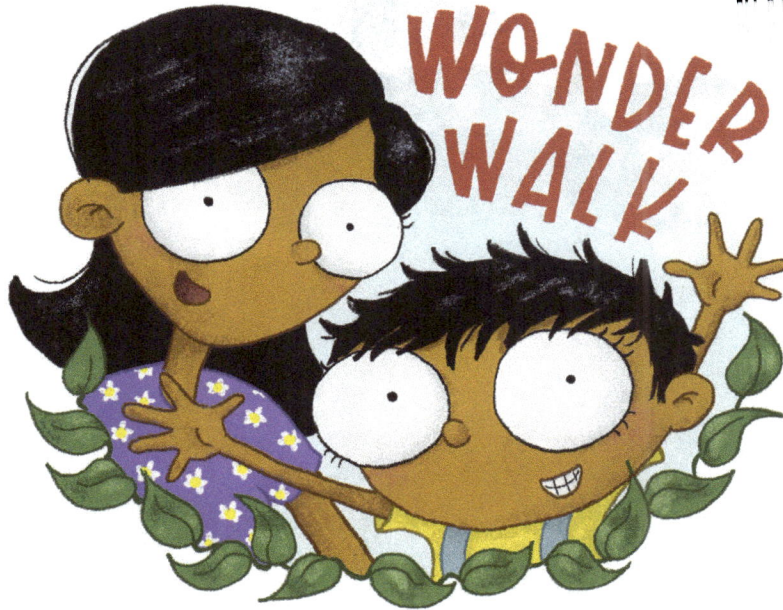

"Dedicated to my family (you know who you are):
we are together, we have everything."

Copyright © 2019 Ilham Alam
Published by Iguana Books
720 Bathurst Street, Suite 303
Toronto, Ontario, Canada
M5S 2R4
All rights reserved.
ISBN: 978-1-77180-307-6
Book design and front-cover image: Kerry Bell
This is an original print edition of Wonder Walk.

IGUANA

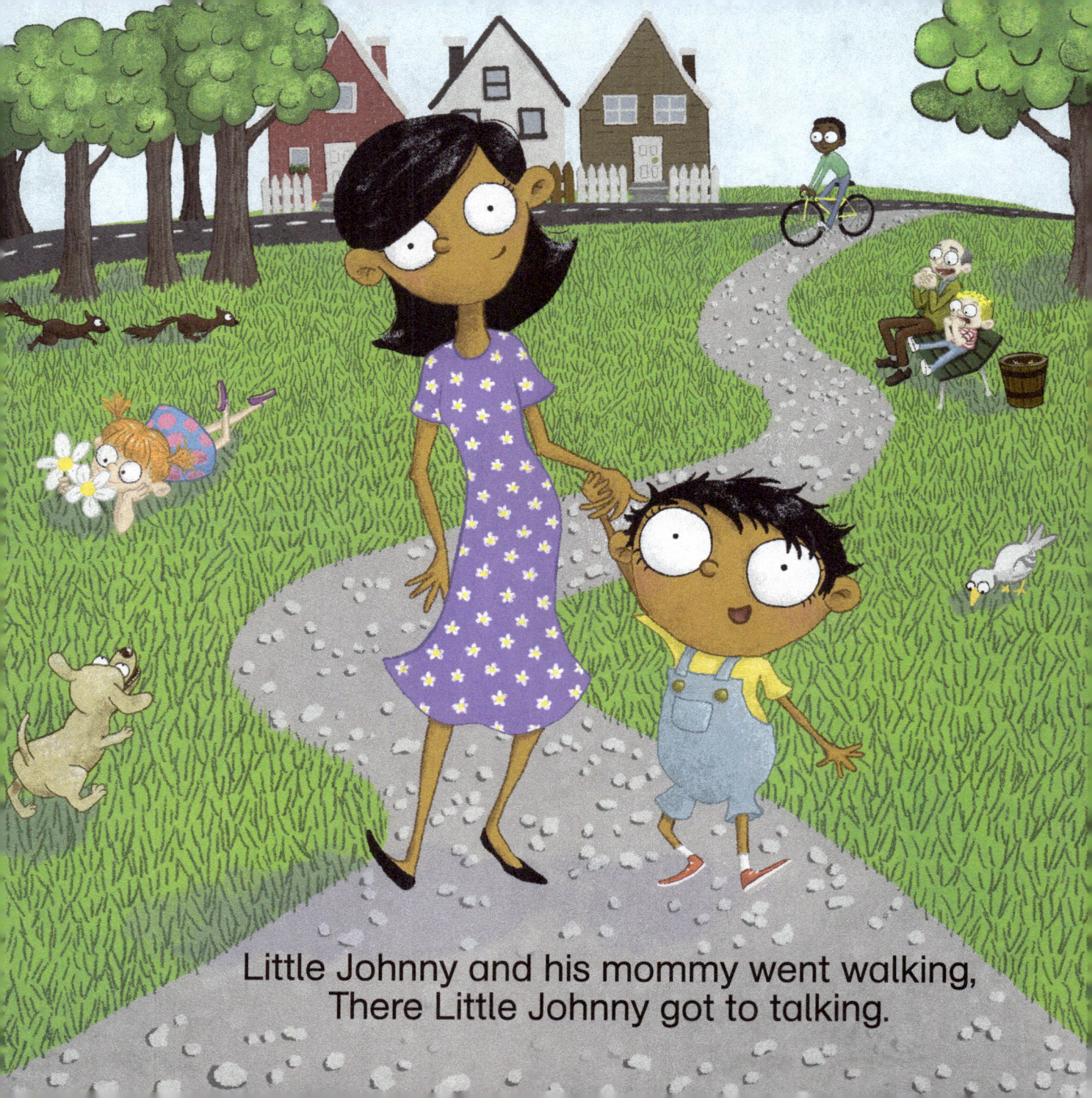

Little Johnny and his mommy went walking,
There Little Johnny got to talking.

"Oh Mommy Mommy!
What is that pretty thing I see?"

"That is a sunflower.
By day it is a yellow so deep,

But by night it goes to sleep."

Johnny and Mommy walked along
in complete quiet,

Until that was broken by Johnny screaming and pointing,
At something far out of sight.
"Ahhhh Mommy Mommy
What is that scary thing I see?"

"Why that must be cuddly cuddle-bug,
Crawling over here to give you a hug.

He wants to wish you goodnight,
And do not let the bed bugs bite!"

"But but mommy?"
"Yes Johnny?"
"Why does the bug say goodnight?
When the sun is out and oh so bright
And the sky is blue?
Doesn't the silly bug have a clue?"

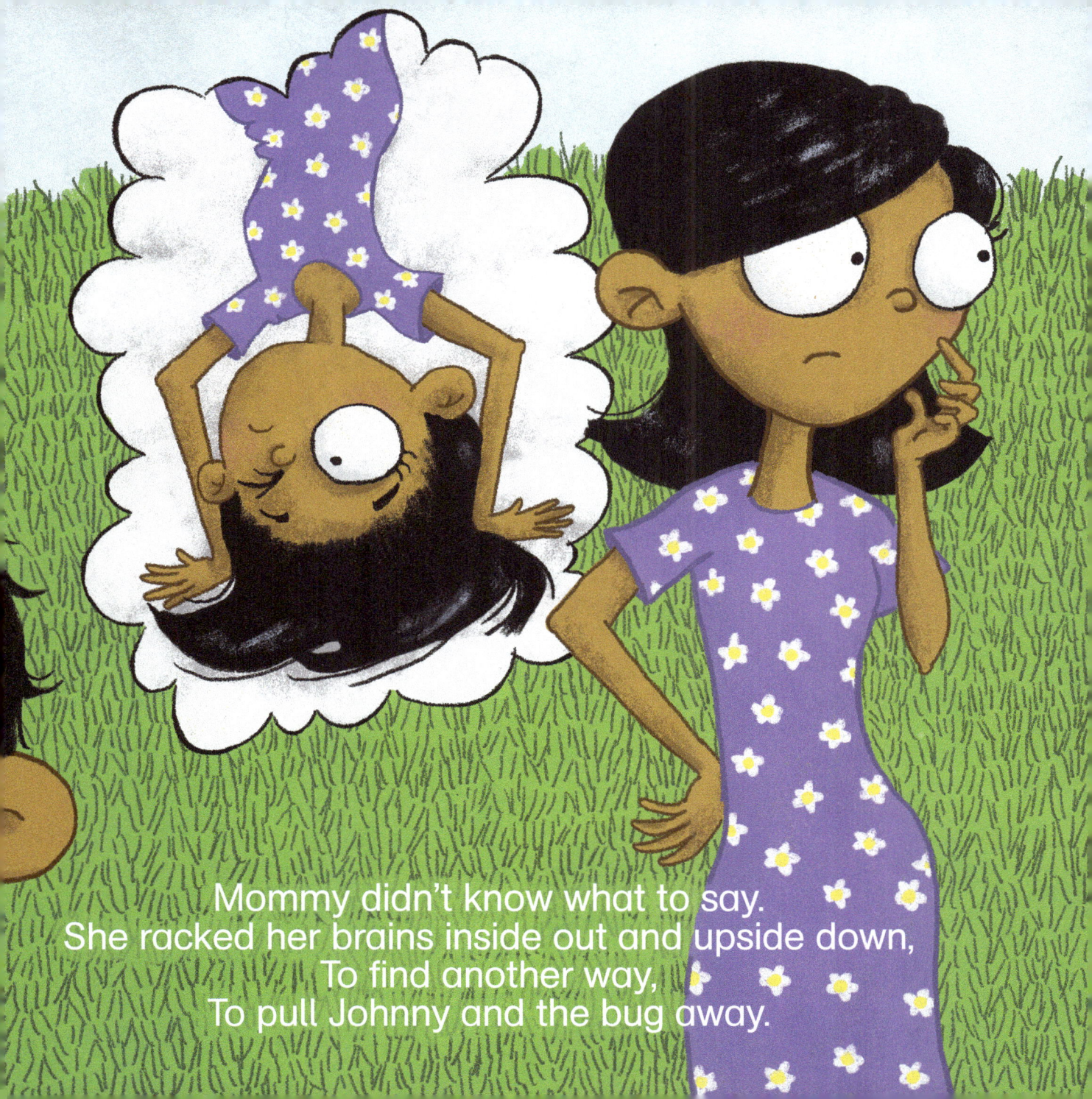

Mommy didn't know what to say.
She racked her brains inside out and upside down,
To find another way,
To pull Johnny and the bug away.

"Oh look my son!
There is a red bird up on that tree,
with her little one.
Come on, come on!
Let us go see, Johnny,
Won't that be fun?"

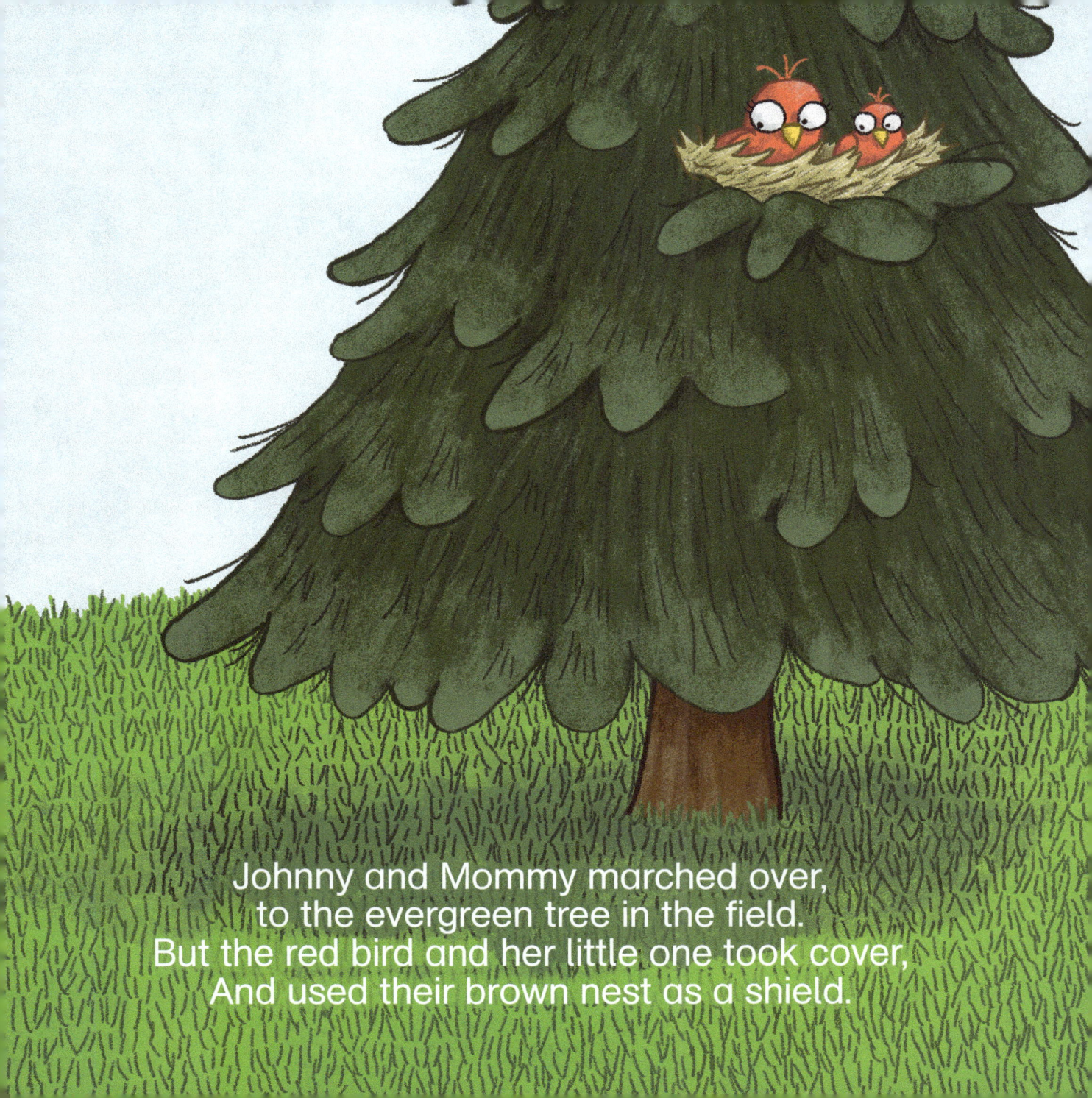

Johnny and Mommy marched over,
to the evergreen tree in the field.
But the red bird and her little one took cover,
And used their brown nest as a shield.

"Why is that bird so shy?
I just wanted to say Hi,
And kiss the baby bird and sing it a song,
that needs to be heard."

"Well, the mommy bird
doesn't want her baby to get hurt.
So she and her baby hid,
and are being curt."

Then Johnny let out a great big
YAWWWN,
And rubbed his eyes.
Mommy ruffled his hair and cried,
"You've been up since dawn so let us go home!
Now say your goodbyes."

Mommy picked up her Johnny,
And carried him all the way home.

Once they entered through the door,
Johnny already was in the world of dreams.
And wanted to dream some more.

If you enjoyed this story, please leave a review on the website where you purchased it and/or on Goodreads. Thank You and hope you enjoyed Wonder Walk.

www.ingramcontent.com/pod-product-compliance
Lightning Source LLC
Chambersburg PA
CBHW041434040426
42452CB00021B/2976